THE GOD IN YOU B~~.~~ ~~~~~~ ~~~~~~ ~~~~~~ SERIES

FULFILLED!
ENJOYING GOD'S
PURPOSE FOR YOU

A Bible Study by

Churches Alive!

MINISTERING TO THE CHURCHES OF THE WORLD
600 Meridian Avenue, Suite 200
San Jose, California 95126-3427

Published by

NAVPRESS
BRINGING TRUTH TO LIFE
NavPress Publishing Group
P.O. Box 35001, Colorado Springs, Colorado 80935

Cover illustration: Catherine Kanner

Scripture quotations are from the *Holy Bible:
New International Version* (NIV). Copyright
© 1973, 1978, 1984, International Bible
Society. Used by permission of Zondervan
Bible Publishers.

Printed in the United States of America

11 12 13 14 15 16 17 18 19 20/99 98 97 96 95

*Because we share kindred aims for helping local churches fulfill Christ's
Great Commission to "go and make disciples," NavPress and Churches
Alive have joined efforts on certain strategic publishing projects that are
intended to bring effective disciplemaking resources into the service of
the local church.*

*For more than a decade, Churches Alive has teamed up with churches of
all denominations to establish vigorous disciplemaking ministries. At
the same time, NavPress has focused on publishing Bible studies, books,
and other resources that have grown out of The Navigators' fifty years of
disciplemaking experience.*

*Now, together, we're working to offer special products like this one that
are designed to stimulate a deeper, more fruitful commitment to Christ
in the local gatherings of His Church.*

The GOD IN YOU Bible Study Series *was written by Russ Korth, Ron
Wormser, Jr., and Ron Wormser, Sr., of Churches Alive. Many individuals from both Churches Alive and NavPress contributed greatly in
bringing this project to publication.*

Contents

About the Author

In your hand you have just one item of a wide range of discipling helps, authored and developed by Churches Alive with one overall, church-centered, biblical concept in mind: GROWING BY DISCIPLING!

Convinced that the local church is the heart of God's plan for the world, a number of Christian leaders joined in 1973 to form Churches Alive. They saw the need for someone to work hand-in-hand with local churches to help them develop fruitful discipleship ministries.

Today, the ministry of Churches Alive has grown to include personal consulting assistance to church leaders, a variety of discipleship books and materials, and training conferences for clergy and laypeople. These methods and materials have proven effective in churches large and small of over 45 denominations.

From their commitment and experience in church ministry, Churches Alive developed the Growing by Discipling plan to help you

- minister to people at their levels of maturity.
- equip people for ministry.
- generate mature leaders.
- perpetuate quality.
- balance growth and outreach.

Every part of Growing by Discipling works together in harmony to meet the diverse needs of people - from veteran church members to the newly awakened in Christ. This discipling approach allows you to integrate present fruitful ministries and create additional ones through the new leaders you develop. This concept follows Christ's disciplemaking example by helping you to meet people at their points of need. Then, you help them build their dependence on God so they experience His love and power. Finally, you equip them to reach out to others in a loving, effective, and balanced ministry of evangelism and helping hands.

Headquartered in San Jose, California, with staff across the United States and in Europe, Churches Alive continues to expand its ministry in North America and overseas.

Introduction

"The one who has the most toys when he dies wins," reads a bumper sticker.

Not true.

Many people look to their toys for fulfillment. They buy cars, boats, and condos. They take trips, cruises, and tours. They may have fun, but not fulfillment.

Others pursue fulfillment in the opposite direction. They become workaholics, losing themselves in their careers. They set goals and manage themselves by their objectives. They may know accomplishment, but not fulfillment.

Fulfillment comes from being in God, from God being in you, and from taking part in His work. He said, "I am your shield, your very great reward" (Genesis 15:1).

HOW TO USE THIS BIBLE STUDY. This book leads you through a unique approach to making the Bible meaningful. In each chapter you will study one passage, not isolated verses, to explore some of the major themes of God's Word. In the process, you'll learn Bible study methods that will be useful for the rest of your life.

You will gain maximum benefit from this book by completing the questions about the study passage and then meeting with a group of people to discuss what you discovered in your study.

No doubt, your group could spend many weeks exploring the richness of just one of these Bible passages. But much greater profit accompanies a pace of one chapter each week. This stride guarantees sustained enthusiasm that will leave people wanting more.

The leader's guide designed for this series aids the group leader in launching and guiding the discussion. It provides help for using the series in a home-study group or a classroom setting.

HINTS TO ENHANCE YOUR EXPERIENCE. The translation used in writing this study is the *New International Version* (NIV) of the Bible. All quotations are from this translation.

Though written using the NIV, this workbook adapts readily to other Bible translations. In fact, it adds interest and variety in group discussions when people use different translations.

Your book includes space to answer each question. But some people choose to mark some of their answers in an inexpensive Bible. Creating a study Bible like this allows a person to benefit from notes and information year after year.

Above all, *use* the insight you gain. The truths of the Bible were not recorded to rest on dusty shelves. God designed them to live in the experiences of people. In preparing this series, the authors never intended merely to increase your intellectual knowledge of the Bible—but to help you put into action the tremendous resources available in Jesus Christ.

"Looks like the pastor needs volunteers."

1.
Offering Yourself

Study passage: Romans 11:33–12:21

Focus: Romans 12:1: Therefore, I urge you, brothers, in view of God's mercy, to offer your bodies as living sacrifices, holy and pleasing to God — which is your spiritual worship.

1 The first portion of this passage describes the One to whom you are to offer yourself. As you learn more about Him, you will gain a greater desire to offer yourself to Him.

Read verses 33-36 each day this week and meditate on them, looking for the meanings, implications, and applications of these statements. Each day, record insights you gain through this activity.

8

Day 1

Day 2

Day 3

Day 4

Day 5

Day 6

Day 7

2 In Romans 12:1 and 2, offering yourself to God is presented as a reasonable conclusion based on the information in chapters 1 through 11. According to the study passage, why should you offer yourself to God?

3 When people offer themselves to God, He enables them to use their gifts to work effectively with others. Verses 3-8 refer to using spiritual gifts in the Church. In your study of these verses, what do you conclude about how to use your gift(s)?

What instruction(s) in this paragraph (verses 3-8) do you think would help a person identify his or her gift(s)?

4 Offering yourself to God creates a desire to fulfill His commands. Read the list of commands in verses 9-16 and ask God to reveal one command you can fulfill this week.

5 The last paragraph of the passage (verses 17-21) gives specific instructions on how to react to those who hurt you. In your own words, briefly tell what you are supposed to do.

Why should you do that?

Why is God responsible to protect from evil all who have offered themselves to Him?

Use the concepts in Romans 12:1-2 to write a prayer of your dedication to God.

"It's a special model for committees. It comes equipped with one gas pedal, 4 steering wheels, and 10 sets of brakes."

2.
Working Together

Study passage: Ephesians 4:1-16

Focus: Ephesians 4:16: From him the whole body, joined and held together by every supporting ligament, grows and builds itself up in love, as each part does its work.

1 A group of individuals (a church) who have obeyed Romans 12:1 and offered themselves to God become effective for Him and enjoy improved relationships with each other. This kind of togetherness is one of the themes of this letter to the Ephesian church, and is essential for churches today if they are to function as God intends. Based on the

study passage, identify the attitudes that enable us to work together.

the ways in which we work together.

the results of working together.

---

2 Oneness (or unity) is a theme of verses 1-6. In your opinion, how would you rate the following aspects of the Christian life for their importance in maintaining unity?

	Unimportant					Very important	
Agreeing on doctrine	0	1	2	3	4	5	6
Attending the same church	0	1	2	3	4	5	6
Overlooking mistakes	0	1	2	3	4	5	6
Using gifts	0	1	2	3	4	5	6
Liking each other	0	1	2	3	4	5	6
Other: _____	0	1	2	3	4	5	6

Choose one aspect that you rated high. What concepts presented in this passage support your conclusion?

3 Considering the context, why do you think Paul makes such a strong appeal for unity in this passage?

4 Another major topic in this passage is growth. What provisions for growth are mentioned in verses 7 and 8?

What process of growth is presented in verses 11-13?

5 As an individual, you are to grow to maturity. How is a mature Christian pictured in this passage?

In what ways do you see yourself as a mature Christian?

In what areas do you need to mature?

---

6 Describe how people are working together in your church to cause spiritual growth.

Describe how you are working with others in your church.

ONE	SOME
● Body	● Apostles
● Spirit	● Prophets
● Hope	● Evangelists
● Lord	● Pastors
● Faith	● Teachers
● Baptism	● Gifts
● God and Father of all	

3.
Helping Others Grow

Study passage: 1 Thessalonians 2:1-12

Focus: 1 Thessalonians 2:8: We loved you so much that we were delighted to share with you not only the gospel of God but our lives as well, because you had become so dear to us.

1 Thessalonica was the largest city in Macedonia, and its capital. It was located on an important harbor for imports and exports, and adjoined one of the main land trade routes. Paul founded the church there. He wrote this letter to the church following Timothy's visit to Thessalonica at Paul's request. In this passage, he reviews with the church how he had helped them.

16

What actions did he take to help them grow?

How did he feel about them?

---

2 Paul referred to his relationship to the believers in terms of a family. In what sense was he their mother (mentioned in verse 7)?

In what sense was he their father (mentioned in verse 11)?

---

3 In helping others to grow, Paul set an example by his life. Acts 16:16-40 describes events in Philippi that preceded Paul's visit to Thessalonica. Acts 17:1-9 gives an account of Paul and his companion Silas in Thessalonica. In these two passages, what character qualities do you see represented in Paul and Silas?

How does Paul describe himself in 1 Thessalonians 2:1-12?

How does his example challenge you?

4 In verse 8, Paul said he communicated more than the right information; he shared his life, also. What do you think is involved in sharing your life with others? (Use ideas from the passage and your own thoughts.)

5 Helping others grow spiritually often comes from assuming a responsibility in your church. Use what you've learned from this passage to write a description of the *ideal* church school teacher, committee member, youth leader, or other discipling leader.

The ideal _____

Training or experience required

Personal qualifications

Responsibilities

For what is our hope, our joy, or the
crown in which we will glory in the presence
of our Lord Jesus when he comes? Is it not you?
Indeed, you are our glory and joy.

Paul, Silas, and Timothy
to the church at Thessalonica
1 Thessalonians 2:19-20

"What do you think? Should we pray or paddle?"

4.
Balancing Your Faith

Study passage: James 2:14-24

Focus: James 2:17: In the same way, faith by itself, if it is not accompanied by action, is dead.

1 Read through the passage until you feel you understand it. What is the main point James is communicating?

What did you observe in the passage that caused you to conclude this was the main point?

Why do you think this is an important subject for Christians?
(If you don't think it is, tell why not.)

2 In what ways do you find yourself like the person
in verses 15 and 16 who did nothing?

3 James cites Abraham as an example of a man who balanced his faith with action. The episode mentioned in
verse 21 is recorded in detail in Genesis 22. Read it to answer
the following questions.

What did God tell Abraham to do? (Genesis 22:2)

Previously, God told Abraham that he would have descendants through Isaac (Genesis 21:12). How did Abraham explain to himself the apparent contradiction of sacrificing Isaac and having descendants through him? (Hebrews 11:17-19)

In your opinion, why was Abraham's action necessary to confirm his faith?

4 In verse 23 of the study passage, James quotes Genesis 15:6 and then states in verse 24, "A person is justified by what he *does* and *not by faith alone.*" Paul also quotes Genesis 15:6 (in Romans 4:3) and says the person who *"does not work* but trusts God, . . . *his faith* is credited as righteousness" (Romans 4:5).

Below are three statements that attempt to reconcile these viewpoints. Choose one (or write one of your own) and tell why you feel it best reconciles the two passages.

   a. James and Paul had two different definitions for the word *faith.*
   b. Paul viewed this subject from God's perspective; James viewed it from a human perspective.
   c. The two men were addressing different audiences with different purposes in mind.
   d.

5 If you believe "Jesus Christ is Lord," what actions will verify your faith?

Faith never stands around with its
hands in its pockets.

"Excuse me, I'd like to volunteer for committee work involving sensitivity and sacrifice in challenging a secularized, value-impoverished society with the radical claims of the gospel. Thursday afternoons are free."

5.
Caring Enough to Act

Study passage: Matthew 25:14-46

Focus: Matthew 25:40: The King will reply, "I tell you the truth, whatever you did for one of the least of these brothers of mine, you did for me."

1 In the first portion of the study passage Jesus relates a parable. In this parable

who does the man going on the journey represent?

who do his servants represent?

on what basis does he assign them responsibility?

2 A talent was a unit of money worth approximately $1,000. Three men were assigned to handle $5,000, $2,000, and $1,000 respectively.

How does the man with $5,000 compare to the man with $2,000?

Alike	Different

How does the man with $5,000 compare to the man with $1,000?

Alike	Different

In your opinion, which man is most likely to mishandle responsibility?

Why do you think this is true?

3 What do you conclude is the main point of the parable?

How should this affect your life?

4 The rest of the passage talks about a judgment. Who is rewarded? Why?

Who is punished? Why?

---

5 According to the passage, when do you have responsibility to act? (Verses 41-45)

---

6 Do you consider the responsibilities listed in verses 42-43 to be "five-talent," "two-talent," or "one-talent" jobs? Why?

---

7 Review the parable of the talents and the teaching on the sheep and the goats. What are the characteristics of someone who doesn't care enough to act?

What are the characteristics of the person who cares enough to act?

"If we stop now, Harold, we'll be late for Bible study!"

"Now, while Brother Watson is finishing his prayer, let's turn to hymn number . . ."

6.
Praying as a Body

Study passage: Acts 12:1-19

Focus: Acts 12:5: So Peter was kept in prison, but the church was earnestly praying to God for him.

1 This study passage records historical facts primarily. The value of studying this kind of passage usually comes from noting the examples to follow or to avoid. First Corinthians 10:6 says, "Now these things [certain Old Testament stories] occurred as examples, to keep us from setting our hearts on evil things."

One of the negative examples in this passage is Herod. What does the passage say about him? In your opinion, what do these facts reveal about his character?

Fact about Herod	His character

Why do you think Herod wanted to please the Jews?

2 The details of a story like this usually add both color and depth. List the details about Peter's incarceration and then tell what they indicate to you.

Details	What they indicate

3 Approximately how long had Peter been in prison when he was freed? What would the minimum time have been? Read the passage carefully; some information for the answer is there. But you will also need to refer to a Bible dictionary or other reference material.

The passage indicates that the church was praying for him this whole time. Why do you think God waited until the day before Peter's trial to free him?

4 The passage does not tell us what the church prayed. What do you think they prayed?

What is revealed about the church's diligence in prayer?

What is revealed about their faith?

5 How is your church like the one in this passage?

How do you think this example from Acts can help you and your church?

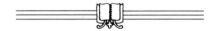

Before they call I will answer;
while they are still speaking I will hear.

God
Isaiah 65:24

"And then, when I was two years old . . ."

7.
Telling Your Story

Study passage: John 9

Focus: John 9:25: He replied, "Whether he is a sinner or not, I don't know. One thing I do know. I was blind but now I see!"

1 When Jesus and the disciples encountered this blind man, the disciples voiced their concern about a point of theology. They wanted to know who was to blame for the man's blindness. Jesus redirected their attention from the problem to the solution by meeting the man's need. After he was healed, he told his story many times.

Find these conversations in the passage and complete the chart on page 35.

34

To whom did he tell his story?	What did he say?	Verse

2 The man was asked several questions about his experience with Jesus. He could not answer some of them.
What didn't the man know?

Verse 12

Verses 24-25

Verses 35-36

Although the man didn't know much about Jesus, he did
have definite ideas about Him. What did he conclude about
Jesus?

Verse 17

3 Even though this man was limited in his understanding of Jesus, his story affected others. What do you think made his story effective?

What elements do you need to make your story effective?

4 Two ways the man presented his story are given below. Follow one of these patterns and briefly write your story.

"I was blind but now I see!"
(verse 25).

"He opened my eyes"
(verse 30).

Pattern:
I was . . .
but now I am . . .

Pattern:
Jesus has done something
wonderful for me.

Tell what you were like before
meeting Jesus and afterward.

Tell one wonderful thing
Jesus has done for you
either in salvation or a
current experience.

5 The former blind man first told his story to his friends and neighbors and then to the council of Pharisees. Your sphere of influence may not reach as far as his did. Specifically, who is in your sphere of influence?

Why should you expect your story to affect others in your sphere of influence?

You yourselves are our letter, written on our hearts, known and read by everybody. You show that you are a letter from Christ, the result of our ministry, written not with ink but with the Spirit of the living God, not on tablets of stone but on tablets of human hearts.

Paul and Timothy writing to
the Corinthian church
2 Corinthians 3:2-3

"Okay, okay. Tell me more about this Christianity of yours."

8.
Telling His Story

Study passage: Romans 10:1-15

Focus: Romans 10:15: And how can they preach unless they are sent? As it is written, "How beautiful are the feet of those who bring good news!"

---

1 The study passage can be divided into three paragraphs — verses 1-4, 5-13, and 14-15. In the first paragraph of this passage (verses 1-4), Paul tells about his society. In the left-hand column of the chart on page 39, list at least four statements he makes about the Israelites or how he related to them. In the right-hand column, list similar conditions in your society.

Paul's statement	Similar condition in my society
They are zealous for God.	*People love to talk about religion.*

---

2 In the second paragraph (verses 5-13), Paul mentions several things involved in communicating Christ's story. What does the passage *say* you must do to be saved?

Explain what you think these statements mean.

From your understanding of the Scriptures, what should you
include when telling Jesus' story?

---

3 The third paragraph of this passage (verses 14-15) begins
with four questions. Give your answers to these questions.

"How, then, can they call on the one they have not
believed in?"

"And how can they believe in the one of whom they have
not heard?"

"And how can they hear without someone preaching
to them?"

"And how can they preach unless they are sent?"

What my answers indicate I should do:

4 Jesus sent His followers to represent Him to others. The "Great Commission" is the name usually given to His directive, recorded in Matthew 28:18-20. Read this commission. What additional insights do you find that will help you tell Jesus' story?

5 What are the next steps you need to take in developing your ability to tell His story? Use the following questions to stimulate your thinking: What opportunities are available to you? What training is available to you? What actions could open opportunities to talk to friends and neighbors?

O Zion, haste, your mission high fulfilling,
Go tell to all the world that God is Light,
That He who made all nations is not willing
One soul should perish, lost in shades of night.
Publish glad tidings, tidings of peace,
Tidings of Jesus—Redemption and release.

Mary Ann Thomson
Hymn

"Well, what did you expect it to say?"

9.
Working Behind the Scenes

Study passage: Acts 6:1-7

Focus: Acts 6:3-4: Brothers, choose seven men from among you who are known to be full of the Spirit and wisdom. We will turn this responsibility over to them and will give our attention to prayer and the ministry of the word.

1 The rapid growth of the new Christian church in Jerusalem brought many ministry opportunities for church leaders. In the study passage, what problem faced the church?

How did the apostles resolve this problem?

What happened as a result of their solution?

2 In considering people for the behind-the-scenes task, what qualities did the apostles consider to be essential?

Are these the qualities people today normally require for a position of food distribution?

Why do you think these qualities are important for behind-the-scenes duties?

3 In the passage, seven men were chosen to work behind the scenes. Of these men, two are mentioned again in the New Testament. Find the passages in Acts that tell about them and briefly describe what they did.

Stephen	Philip

From your experience, in what ways do you think working behind the scenes prepared them to do these other ministries?

How has working behind the scenes prepared you for other ministry responsibilities?

4 Imagine that you are one of the other five people chosen to "wait on tables." You do not have an opportunity for another ministry but continue in this job for several years. How do you feel

about your position?

about your church?

about yourself?

What is one verse that encourages you to continue to do a good job?

5 List some of the behind-the-scenes jobs in your church and the people doing them. What can you do to encourage them?

Job	Person	Encouragement

The world doesn't need a definition of Christianity
as much as it needs a demonstration.

"This all went so smoothly that I've just decided to make this dinner a weekly event!"

10.
Serving 'Til It Hurts

Study passage: Mark 10:23-45

Focus: Mark 10:43-44: Not so with you. Instead, whoever wants to become great among you must be your servant, and whoever wants to be first must be slave of all.

---

1 After reading verses 23-27, what thoughts and emotions do you think Peter had that caused him to say in verse 28, "We have left everything to follow you"?

What did Jesus promise to people who serve 'til it hurts?
(Verses 29-31)

If a person has complete confidence in Jesus' promise, how
do you think it will affect his or her life and service?

---

2 After this conversation, some of the people were astonished and others were afraid (verse 32). What do you
think caused them to react in these ways?

Jesus took the Twelve aside to tell them He would die. It is
very possible the others heard about it later. How do you
think Jesus' prediction affected

the astonished?

the afraid?

3 Think of the request of James and John as a prayer. In what way(s) was it a good prayer?

In what way(s) was it a bad prayer?

How does considering their "prayer" help you in your prayer life?

4 Jesus did not indicate James and John could have their request. Instead, He told them what they should be doing now. Why do you think it is difficult for a person to follow Jesus' teaching in verses 43 and 44?

5 Those who serve others appear to many people to be servants and nothing more. In the study passage, find as much evidence as possible to support the statement, "Things are not always what they seem to be."

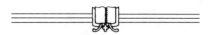

What jobs in your church would everyone like to delegate to a robot?	Following your study of this passage, how should you personally be involved with these jobs?

"Baaahrrrrimmmmmstoneuh . . .!"

11.
Qualifying as a Leader

Study passage: 1 Timothy 3

Focus: 1 Timothy 3:1: Here is a trustworthy saying: If anyone sets his heart on being an overseer, he desires a noble task.

1 The passage refers to two different leadership positions, overseer (bishop or elder) and deacon. Define these two terms.

2 List the requirements for being an overseer, given in verses 2 and 3.

Three other requirements are stated in verses 4-7, along with an explanation for each one. List these requirements and tell why each is important.

Requirement	Why it is important

Put an asterisk (*) by each item in the above list that is a mark of maturity for all Christians.

3 Using the information above, describe a system to evaluate a prospective overseer. If the system includes an interview, tell what questions you would ask.

4 What are the requisites for deacons? (Verses 8, 9, and 12)

What are the requisites for deacons' wives? (Verse 11)

Verse 10 says prospective deacons must first be tested. What do you think is a good test for them?

5 Compare the lists you made in exercises 2 and 4. What do you conclude are some of the major differences between overseers and deacons?

6 After telling the qualifications for being a leader, Paul makes six terse statements about Jesus Christ in verse 16. Why do you think Paul included these in this passage?

7 You have an opportunity to influence others. As you review the qualifications for having leadership responsibilities, what do you consider to be the next step in your development as a leader?

No one from the east or the west
or from the desert can exalt a man.
But it is God who judges:
He brings one down, he exalts another.

A psalm of Asaph
Psalm 75:6-7

"Our choice seems to be between sending a missionary and installing new carpeting in the catacombs."

12.
Reaching to Other Nations

Study passage: Acts 11

Focus: Acts 11:18: When they heard this, they had no further objections and praised God, saying, "So then, God has even granted the Gentiles repentance unto life."

1 With the stoning of Stephen, the Jerusalem church began suffering great persecution. As a result, believers were scattered throughout Judea and Samaria. Wherever they went, they told others about Jesus, the Christ, and how He rose from the dead. Thus, they reached to other nations.

The events in the life of the Apostle Peter recorded in this passage helped to encourage this outreach beyond the Jewish people. What was the vision Peter had in a trance?

What did this mean to Peter?

---

2 In verses 1-3, how was the prejudice toward Gentiles revealed?

How did Peter's audience react after hearing his explanation? (Verse 18)

What does this imply about these people?

Does prejudice affect our reaching to other nations today? Explain your answer.

3 Read verses 19-30 of the study passage and mark on the map the areas mentioned. Next to each location, tell what happened.

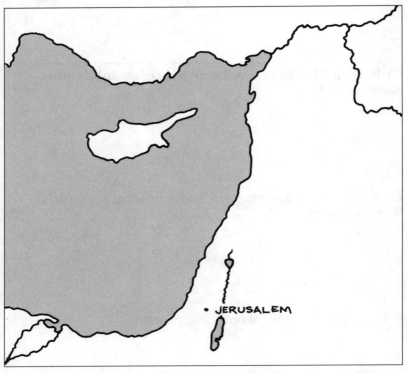

• JERUSALEM

"But you will receive power when the Holy Spirit comes on you; and you will be my witnesses in Jerusalem, and in all Judea and Samaria, and to the ends of the earth." (Acts 1:8)

To you, what is the significance of what was taking place?

4 This chapter includes a good example of how parts of the Body work together to reach other nations. Complete the chart on page 57, referring both to Ephesians 4:11-12 and the study passage.

In principle, what he/they did	Position he/they had (Ephesians 4:11-12)	Person/people named
		Peter
		Men from Cyprus and Cyrene
		Barnabas and Saul
		Agabus

5 What evidence indicates that a strong church had been established at Antioch?

After the church was firmly established, what happened next? (Acts 13:1-3)

What does this imply to you about reaching out to other nations?

6 Peter took steps toward reaching the whole world when he talked to one other person interested in hearing about Jesus. What are some ways for you to become personally involved in reaching out to other nations?

Peter, Stephen, Barnabas, Saul, Agabus—
these men did not collect toys. No vain
pursuits filled their lives.

Though you may not go to a far land or stand
before the masses as these men did, they are still
models of fulfilled lives for you. They were
involved in God's plan and in His work.

Because of **Jesus**, you have God in you. He
has made you **alive**, **rich**, and **powerful**.
You are changed and are fully equipped
to live your life **fulfilled** in God.

Now to him who is able to establish you by my
gospel and the proclamation of Jesus Christ,
according to the revelation of the mystery hidden
for long ages past, but now revealed and made
known through the prophetic writings by the
command of the eternal God, so that all nations
might believe and obey him—to the only wise
God be glory forever through Jesus Christ! Amen.
(Romans 16:25-27)

Developing Lifelong Study Skills

The variety of methods you followed to complete the study are skills you can use throughout your life to understand and apply other passages in the Bible.

This summary identifies a few of the skills covered in this book, and will serve as a helpful guide for your future Bible study.

1. MEDITATING. Meditating is the act of contemplating, or thinking carefully. It is usually used in conjunction with other study methods, but in chapter 1 you read a portion of the study passage every day for a week and meditated on it. It is an art developed by practice.

2. EVALUATING. Using the Bible to evaluate situations and circumstances often will lead you to new understanding or to appropriate applications. In chapter 2 you used Ephesians 4 to evaluate how well six activities help maintain unity. When you study a passage, make a list of common ideas, traditions, and cliche's that relate to the subject of the passage. Then use what you learn from the Bible to evaluate these items.

3. CORRELATING. Correlation is bringing two ideas or related topics together into one comprehensive view. Sometimes a passage will bring out only one side of an issue. You need to consider the teachings of other passages to gain a balanced and complete understanding. For example, in chapter 4 you examined statements by James (in James 2:23) and Paul (in Romans 4:3) regarding faith and works. By correlating these statements, you can avoid an extremism that might otherwise result.

4. ADDING BACKGROUND. Some statements in the Bible will make sense to you only after you add background information. For example, in chapter 6 you were asked to determine the approximate length of time Peter spent in prison. The passage states he was imprisoned during the Feast of Unleavened Bread and released at the end of the Passover. You need the background information about these events to answer the question. Usually, you can find this kind of information in a Bible dictionary or Bible encyclopedia.